TJ'S Then & Now
How Trader Joe's Changed the Way America Eats

(an unauthorized culinary history)

Susie Wyshak
Oakland, California

This book is an independent work. It is not affiliated with, sponsored by, approved, or endorsed by the Trader Joe's Company.

Contact: Susie Wyshak, P.O. Box 5448, Berkeley, CA 94705
susie@foodstarter.com

ISBN-10: 0-9967017-1-0
ISBN-13: 978-0-9967017-1-6

Dedication

To Dad, who introduced me to my love of Trader Joe's®.
To the staff who welcomed Mom to adventure the aisles.
To Trader Joe's, which has been such a big part of my happy life.

Acknowledgements

Thank you for the contributions of these talented folk:

Design & illustrations: Joshua Lagman (lazanalagman.weebly.com)
Editing: Cathy Luchetti, Robin Wyshak, Jeanne Wyshak, and my food professional friends who shared invaluable feedback and stories as the book came together.

This Book Does Good

A portion of profits from this book will be donated to food banks and to the non-profit Daily Table grocery store.

Table of Contents

A Food Treasure Unearthed

We all yearn for that once-in-a-lifetime Indiana Jones moment, that one where you find a masterpiece at a garage sale or a saber tooth in the backyard. My Jones moment occurred one day in 2015, in a dark garage in Los Angeles.

I'd been poking around the glovebox of our family's old car. The car had been parked for decades, covered with enough dust to impress an Indiana Jones special-effects team.

The glovebox was nearly empty. No car manual. No registration papers. Just a yellowed, folded Trader Joe's newsletter. I carefully pulled the flyer from the glove compartment and opened it. The pages began crumbling with each turn.

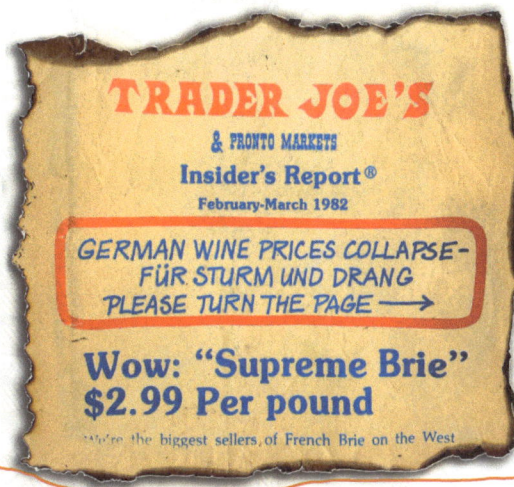

TRADER JOE'S
& PRONTO MARKETS
Insider's Report ®
February-March 1982

GERMAN WINE PRICES COLLAPSE—
FÜR STURM UND DRANG
PLEASE TURN THE PAGE ⟶

Wow: "Supreme Brie"
$2.99 Per pound

We're the biggest sellers of French Brie on the West

My eyes widened. This 1982 relic was no *Fearless Flyer.* The pre-"Trader Joe's" name of "Pronto Markets" hadn't been totally phased out….and the Fearless Flyer name hadn't been phased in.

Perhaps the flyer had come from my first Trader trip, that day Dad told the young me to pile into the car for a shopping trip to Pasadena. At the time, the idea

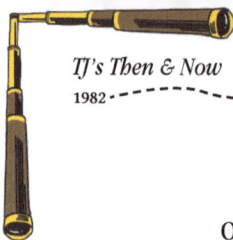

of driving 20+ miles across Los Angeles for a few small purchases seemed kind of weird. All that way? For what? Jagermeister and chocolate mints.

Dad didn't explain quite why we needed to go *there* for *that*. All I knew was that he couldn't resist a bargain.[1] If Dad would spend gas money—at 8 miles per gallon—this store must have some awesome bargains.

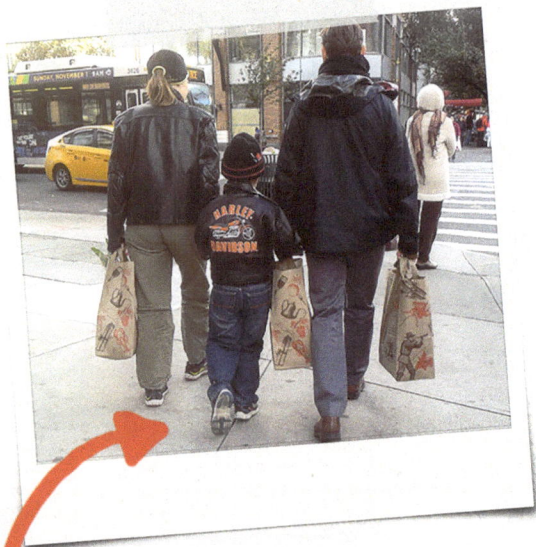

Do you remember your first Trader?

Share your memories of discovering Trader Joe's at TraderJoesHistory.com

This Book is a Tribute To Trader Joe's

I've tracked down TJ's on road trips, thrown countless TJ-themed parties, and visited the store just for kicks. What would life be without Trader Joe's? I can't imagine either.

Reading the 1982 flyer, I noticed many "new" foods that we now couldn't live without. The story of how TJ's led us to new and healthier food territories had to be told.

Like an archaeological dig, this book offers a peek into how different the world of food was a mere 35 years ago. As you dig into this flyer, you'll discover Trader Joe's pioneering role in making new and exotic foods part of our daily diets. The flyer crumbled as I scanned it. You'll have to fill in some blanks, like a TJ's archaeologist.

Writing *TJ's Then & Now* has made me a bigger fan than ever. I hope you enjoy it, too.

- Susie Wyshak

---

[1] Old-time LA folks remember FEDCO, the original membership bargain store. We were die-hard FEDCO shoppers.

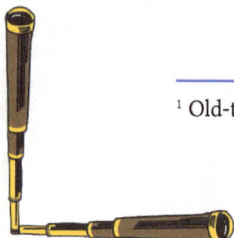

Trader Joe's was not a household name, but a store that foodies went to, long before they were even called "foodies."

Back in 1982, Trader Joe's was 15 years old with only 16 stores, all in Southern California. (Now 450+ stores across the United States have made TJ's a household name.)

Most big cities had "gourmet" and international food stores. But just as most corner liquor stores didn't become chains, most of those international stores had just one, or a few, shops. Trader Joe's took the helm to bring healthy, adventurous food to the masses.

When Dad heard I was writing this book, he flashed back to that time he landed a case of half-pint-sized, 12-year old scotch at the Eagle Rock Trader Joe's. Memories might fade, but bargain hunters never forget.

You had to call a store for directions—or maybe stores directed you, as TJ's did for Cal-State Fullerton students.

I have complete confidence in Trader Joe — and all his branches!

THE BRANCHES OF TRADER JOE

Orange County

Fullerton, 1700 N. Placentia Ave.	(714) 528-9491	528-9496
Santa Ana, 1303 North Main	(714) 558-9843 - 558-9641	—
Costa Mesa, 103 E. 17th (West of Newport Blvd. — near Superior Blvd.)	(714) 631-9383	631-9391

West Side & South Bay

W. Los Angeles, 10850 National Blvd.	474-9289 - 474-9018	
Westchester, 8645 S. Sepulveda	642-8794	642-8923
Manhattan Beach, 1821 Manhattan Beach Blvd.	374-9540-374-9337	—

San Fernando Valley - Glendale

Encino, 17640 Burbank Blvd.	995-9571 - 995-9521	
Sherman Oaks, Riverside Dr. & Hazeltine	995-9349	995-9486
Eagle Rock, 1566 Colorado Blvd.	256-9387	256-9247
La Crescenta, 3433 Foothill Blvd.	248-9749 - 248-9994	

West San Gabriel Valley

Pasadena, 610 S. Arroyo Pkwy.	578-9540 - 356-9066	578-9450
East Pasadena, 311 S. Rosemead	578-9263	356-9160
Alhambra, 701 S. Atlantic Blvd.	576-9474	576-9570
South Pasadena, 613 Mission St.	799-9293	799-3849
Monterey Park, 1800 W. Garvey	576-9302	—

PRONTO MARKETS

		Sandwich Shops
Monrovia, 227 E. Foothill Blvd.	359-9978	359-9829
Highland Park, 623 North Ave. 64	256-9890	
Culver City, 10045 Culver Blvd.	558-9225	558-9062
West Covina, 220 South Citrus	331-9842	

The date on the *Insider Report* is just a way of referencing it. We don't change our prices, unless our costs change. The prices in this Report will not necessarily expire at the end of March. If we still have supplies, at the same costs, in April — our retail will remain the same. More commonly, we have sold out our entire supply of any given item, long before the next issue of the *Insider* appears. The next issue of the *Insider* will be mailed about April 1.

If you attend Cal-State Fullerton, our closest store is on Placentia Ave. just south of Yorba Linda Blvd.

Note to Youngsters:

To enhance your time travel, picture this: Whole Foods had just one store in Austin, Texas. Costco had yet to be founded.

Word got around by phone (the kind plugged into a wall, with a dial or push buttons), by mail (letters!), and with those "You'll never guess what I found..." conversations in person.

The World Wide Web would not exist for 10+ years. Computers, e-mail and online chat rooms were a secret world known only to super techies— like the folks at Caltech in Pasadena, where Trader Joe's first opened shop.

Microwaves were rare. Rumor had it they leaked waves and could kill you. Convenience vs. death. Hmm.

Even in 1986, *only about 25 percent* of U.S. households owned a microwave oven.[2] This explains the absence of microwaveable meals in this flyer. Can you imagine?

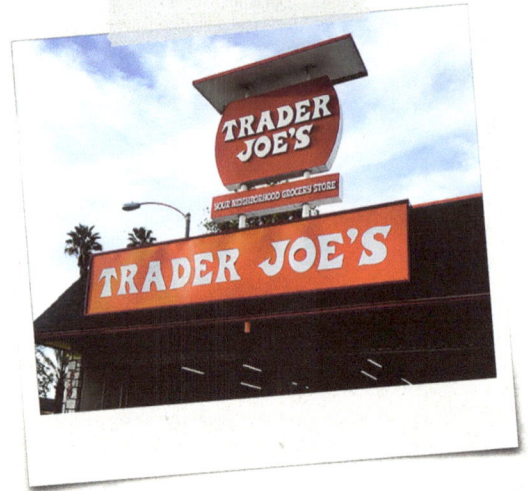

---

[2] The IEEE (The Institute of Electrical and Electronics Engineers), A History of the Microwave Oven, http://theinstitute.ieee.org/tech-history/technology-history/a-history-of-the-microwave-oven

The flyer reveals just how important Trader Joe's has been in creating a generation of fearless foodies.

Skip ahead to the flyer (page 12) or read on for some backstory on what's different, and the same, about this young 1982 Trader Joe's.

It's a Real Page-Turner.

Within the rollicking writing, you'll see the company's genuine concern for the physical and financial health of customers, while inspiring us to explore new, more interesting, and better foods.

Typical store flyers, newspaper ads, and catalogs were all about sale prices, features, and buy buy buy. Trader Joe's had something different in mind when the first customer newsletter came out in 1970: **Educate, entice,** **and make strange, new foods sound not so strange—and irresistible.** In other words, turn customers into food adventurers, just like the "Trader," founder Joe Coulombe.

What they called "The Insider Report" was a big hit; the company timeline[3] recalls that customers coveted the newsletter so much they even paid for it.

Did book clubs form around reading the newsletter? Maybe not, but you can bet a lot of people passed along the tidbits they read…and word got around.

We Get Hints About Typical Old-Time TJ's Customers.

Long-time shoppers often remember trekking to distant cities with Trader Joe's

---

[3] TraderJoes.com http://www.traderjoes.com/our-story/timeline

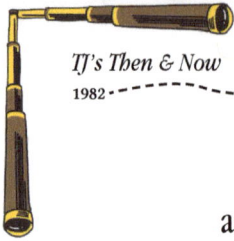

as the destination. You'd call the store for directions, slowly peruse the aisles, then eagerly report your finds to friends. Those friends in Trader-less territory would inevitably beg, entice, or downright order friends to make deliveries.

Coulombe explained how he chose the store locations: "All Trader Joe's were located near centers of learning… for overeducated and underpaid people." He picked Pasadena for the first location, which he called "the epitome of a well-educated town."[4] (Trivia for *Big Bang Theory* fans: He was most likely referring to Caltech University. Keep this in mind as you read the product descriptions full of brainiac tidbits.)

Trader Joe's fame for low-priced gourmet foods was matched by their real estate know-how: They chose locations that were cheap and off-the-beaten-path properties, yet close enough to affluent communities for good business traffic.[5] Pasadena, for example, is about 10-20 miles from more populated, wealthy parts of Los Angeles. Not very close, but not too far.

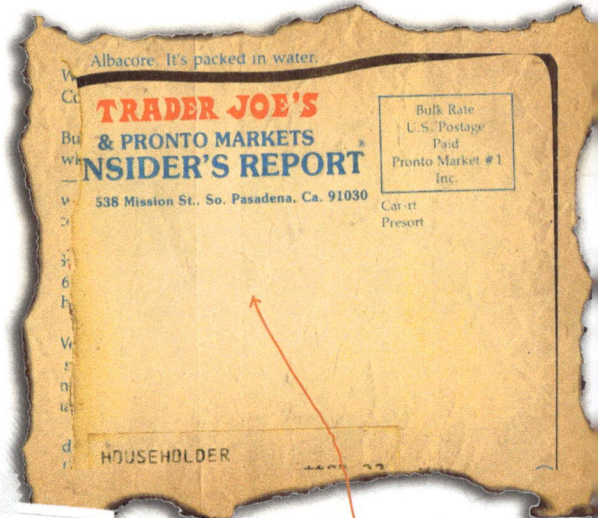

Albacore. It's packed in water.

TRADER JOE'S
& PRONTO MARKETS
NSIDER'S REPORT
538 Mission St.. So. Pasadena. Ca. 91030

Bulk Rate
U.S. Postage
Paid
Pronto Market #1
Inc.

Ca..rt
Presort

HOUSEHOLDER

NOW: Some of Trader Joe's busiest stores are sandwiched between some of the nation's most expensive real estate in big cities like New York and San Francisco.

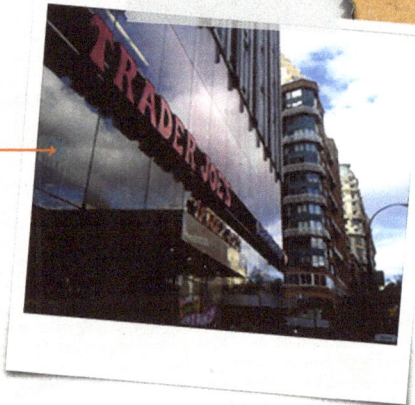

THEN: Trader Joe's began in the quiet, relatively old California town of Pasadena, known for brainy people and little old ladies (thanks to a famous Beach Boys song).

---

[4] Patt Morrison, "Joe's Joe: Joe Coulombe", *Los Angeles Times* http://articles.latimes.com/2011/may/07/opinion/la-oe-morrison-joe-coulombe-043011 (May 7, 2011)

[5] A 2015 study by Zillow.com even found that real estate values increase more for homes are near Trader Joe's vs. Whole Foods. (Maybe homes near Whole Foods were already higher priced, since Whole Foods Markets tend to locate in affluent areas. Or maybe the love of Trader is just that strong.) See: http://zillow.mediaroom.com/2016-01-25-Homes-Near-Trader-Joes-Whole-Foods-Stores-Appreciate-Faster

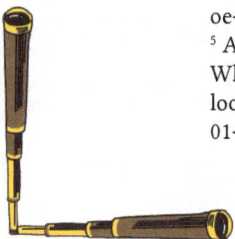

The Flyer Names Names!

A 2010 article in *Fortune Magazine* says that Trader Joe's wants neither its shoppers nor its competitors to know who's making its products.[6]

It was a different story when the company had just a few locations. Back then, TJ's could more easily distribute lots of very small batches of foods and drinks to all of the stores—and promote them in the flyer.

Why They Don't Name Names Now

Lots of supermarkets sell products under their special store brand, keeping the names of manufacturers they may hire to make those goods a secret. This makes sense. Customers will turn to your company to buy the stuff they love.

In honor of this practice, some supplier names on the 1982 flyer are blacked out or omitted (even though those companies may not still be supplying TJ's).

The Flyer Has Screaming Limited-Edition "Flash" Sales.

"When it's gone, it's gone!" Talk about a smart way to get people buying and coming back to see what's new—just like today's online flash sales.

Joe Coulombe explained the concept of selling limited lots:

"…we deliberately pursued a policy of discontinuity, as opposed to, say, Coca-Cola, which is in infinite supply. For example, we had the only vintage-dated, field-specific canned corn in existence, and it was the best damned canned corn there was. But there was only so much produced every year, and when you're out, you're out." [7]

[6] Beth Kowitt, "Inside the Secret World of Trader Joe's", *Fortune*
http://archive.fortune.com/2010/08/20/news/companies/inside_trader_joes_full_version.fortune/index.htm#joe (August 23, 2010)
[7] ibid

A Simpler Time for Food

Imagine walking into the average grocery store and not being able to walk out with:

- ready-to-eat salads, sandwiches and wraps (though TJ's customers recall deli service in some early locations)
- tubs of hummus
- a million yogurt choices
- snack bars galore. (Aside from Tiger Milk Bars and Nature Valley Granola Bars, snack bars were minimal. Power Bar didn't come along till 1986. Clif? 1992!)
- frozen meals that weren't "TV dinners"
- pre-cooked packaged rice, Indian food…

You get the picture — a lot less choice than we have today.

We didn't know what we were missing. People cooked at home, ordered take out or dropped by a fast food joint, pizzeria or anything in between. (This was way before Chipotle, Panera, and the whole "fast casual" trend in health-oriented chain restaurants.)

Back in the 80s, the words "authenticity" and "transparency" were not part of food promotion. People didn't obsess about where their food came from. We trusted the brands behind the food. We really came to trust Trader Joe's. The stories behind the food you'll read about were a big reason TJ's earned (and kept) our trust!

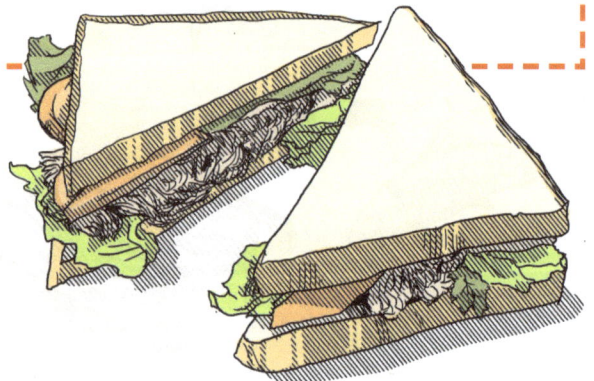

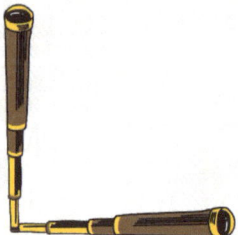

The Time Was Right

Jonathan Kauffman, author of *Hippie Food: How Back-to-the-Landers, Longhairs, and Revolutionaries Changed the Way We Eat*, explains why it makes sense that health food arose in the late 1960s:

"Young customers who had read Silent Spring and muckraking books exposing the possible effects of consuming food additives, not to mention a flurry of scandals about pesticide contamination, were beginning to demand transparency from their food supply. They attempted to return to a time before processed food had taken over the American diet, and sought out whole, unprocessed products from sources they trusted. Aesthetically, they privileged the ramshackle and the unstudied over the slick and corporate. And despite their focus on small-scale and local, they traveled abroad more widely than their parents and grandparents, and adopted foods from unfamiliar cuisines quite readily."

Trader Joe's was just the ticket.

How Trader Joe's Struck Gold

'Twas 1970. Trader Joe's was still a wee company when Coulombe noticed the word "biosphere" in Scientific American. The importance of food being natural and pure struck Coulombe. From that one article, he decided Trader Joe's should focus on healthier, more environmental options.[8]

Trader Joe's wove a killer formula of quality guarantees and trust, which leads us to happily fork over billions of dollars a year for Trader Joe's store-brand products (also known as "private label" products).

You'll see how sincere TJ's commitment to quality has always been as you embark on your flyer time travel…

[8] Beth Kowitt, "Meet the Original Joe", Fortune.com
http://features.blogs.fortune.cnn.com/2010/08/23/meet-the-original-joe/?iid=EL (August 23, 2010)

Wild & Wonderful Foods

Picture yourself reading this flyer for the first time, learning about most of these foods for the first time

A Cheesy Adventure

Take us away, Trader Joe's!

TJ's Re-defined "American Cheese"

While millions of households sprayed cheese on Nachos, melted processed American cheese slices onto burgers, and shook parmesan cheese from green cans, the rest of the Western world sliced, melted, and crumbled exotic, flavorful cheeses which they ate for breakfast or for dessert.

You want goat brie?
How about 5-year-old Gouda?
Or truffle-infused cheddar?

You'd have been out of luck in 1982. Even at specialty cheese shops, Limburger, cow's-milk brie, and blue cheese were the gourmet imported cheeses of choice—despite Limburger's notorious smell (quite similar to a humorous bodily function).

This doesn't mean America wasn't big into cheese. Even in the early 80s, American cheese makers were cranking out several billion pounds of cheese per year.[9] Most came from California, Wisconsin, and other pockets of the United States, where immigrant families had imported old-country know-how to make Swiss- and Gouda-like cheeses here on American soil, starting back in the 1800s.

These weren't like those aged Comte and Gruyère cheeses you now find at Trader Joe's. Flavors were milder.

Yes, the Marin French Cheese Company had been making yummy Brie and Camembert since 1865 (known as

---

[9] International Dairy Foods Assocation, http://www.idfa.org/news-views/media-kits/cheese/history-of-cheese

the Rouge et Noir brand). But "artisan" cheese had yet to become a movement... and most of us didn't have a taste for such exotic cheeses—yet. In fact, not until 1980 did Laura Chenel's fresh American-made chèvre goat cheese become a fixture at Berkeley's trend-setting Chez Panisse restaurant.

Let's put it another way. A mere 30 cheese makers entered the American Cheese Society's first competition in 1985. Fast forward to 2016—a whopping 260 American cheese companies entered the competition. Cheeseheads unite![10]

Just Say No To Rennet!

Non-vegetarians might wonder what the fuss is about cheese made with rennet from cow parts. After all, milk is technically a cow by-product. Still, for many ovo-lacto vegetarians, rennet is a no-no.

While Southern California certainly had its share of bran muffin-eating hippies and health fanatics, vegetarianism was definitely not a mainstream diet. Health food was a niche lifestyle, mostly in rural areas and hippie lands like coastal California (See: *Annie Hall*).

While most Americans were buying whatever cheese the supermarkets offered, readers of the Trader Joe's flyer were learning the intricacies of cheese making, sparking customer desire for excellent cheese—hold the cow's stomach lining, thank you very much.

Bombs Away on Rennetless Cheese Price
All Varieties $1.99 Per Pound

Last autumn we introduced Rennetless Cheese — that cheese which is curdled with vegetable substances stead of Rennet (the substance taken from the lining cows' stomachs). We had a great success at $2.49 pound — because the same cheese is sold elsewhere $4.25 per pound!

Now, however, we can break the price to $1.99 per pou — for Rennetless Cheddar, Longhorn and Monte Jack. We have only 15,000 pounds at this special pr Sorry, at this low price we cannot offer the 10% disco on 10 pound chunks.

Today that mysterious "vegetable substance" of which they speak is called "microbial rennet."

[10] American Cheese Society, http://www.cheesesociety.org/about-us/history/

Brie Oh My!

Do you remember your first brie?

Ah, that sophisticated cheese, sometimes a tad stinky, with that weird crust. It was the perfect cheese to whip out at a cocktail party and watch people cut the soft, creamy middle out, leaving the rind for those people arriving fashionably late.

Thanks to irresistible flyer descriptions like the one you see here, Trader Joe's made French Brie an American staple.

*Even 35 years later, Trader has the **very same** French Supreme brie.*

Wow: "Supreme Brie" $2.99 Per pound

We're the biggest sellers of French Brie on the West Coast. We have the lowest price: $3.29 per pound now.

But here comes a shipment of "Supreme" Brie — a cheese which normally retails for over five dollars in the supers — which we can sell for only $2.99 (and if you buy a whole wheel, of course you earn our 10 percent discount).

Supreme Brie is only slightly higher in butterfat content (72%) than the 60% Brie which we normally sell. Why, then, are people willing to pay such a premium for it?

Well, Supreme Brie probably shouldn't be called Brie. It is soft ripened cheese, like Brie, that is in the same flavor and texture spectrum as Brie, but it is made in a different manner.

It doesn't come in wheels but in four pound ovals, and it is thicker than brie. These physical differences, plus differences in the way the milk is handled, result in a profoundly richer, more subtle cheese.

We have only 16000 pounds — we urge you to snap this up and hold it in your freezer!

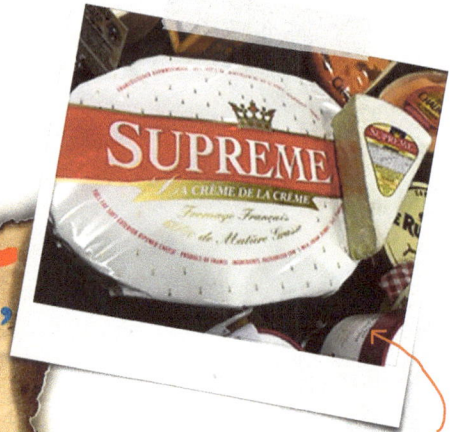

Sure, now it's $9.99 a pound.... still a whole lot cheaper than a trip to France!

FRENCH FONTINA
$1.99 Pound

We introduced this cheese last October, and sold out eight tons almost at once. Our re-order has now arrived from France — we have 10 tons for only $1.99 per pound.

Fontina, one of the best known Italian cheeses, has been copied in many other countries. Most "Fontina" sold here comes from Denmark. The supers sell it for about $3.69 per pound.

France, however, also produces excellent Fontina — and our price of $1.99 is absolutely outstanding. Buy a whole five pound loaf, and save another 10%.

From Fontina to Swiss

Imagine 16,000 pounds of Fontina. That's right, 8 tons of this perfect sandwich-cheese newly arrived at TJ's, the flyer announces. In 1982, you could have loaded up on a jumbo 5-pound brick, enough to feed your family's cheese cravings for weeks—for less than $10. Notice the offer of an extra 10% off, to boot!

SWISS CHEESE FROM FRANCE $1.99 Pound

Switzerland and France share the same mountain ranges, the Alps and the Jura, and both produce remarkably similar cheeses.

So here's a "Swiss" Cheese from France. It has the typical "eyes," with a full, clean flavor. Unlike some "Swiss" cheese, it has a low acid level, making it very agreeable in the mouth.

We're selling this fine cheese for only $1.99 per pound — cheaper than the supers sell "Swiss" from Wisconsin. Buy a whole, three pound wheel — and save another 10 percent!

French Swiss Cheese?!

Trader also landed a Swiss-style cheese from France. The flyer explains explains this oddity: The Alps mountain range, home to amazing cheese, is shared between the two countries.

Note how the flyer elevates customer knowledge, with a scientific note that the "low acid level" makes this cheese tasty. Do you feel smarter already?

Again, TJ's managed to sell at the super low price of $1.99 per pound, then sweetening the deal with 10% off on 3-pound wheel. Fondue time!

Buying massive amounts of cheese in bulk is good for everyone:

1. It costs less to ship as big chunks instead small, wrapped pieces.
2. Cutting as close as possible to selling keeps the cheese fresher.
3. TJ's has the flexibility to cut it, price it, and label it however they wish.

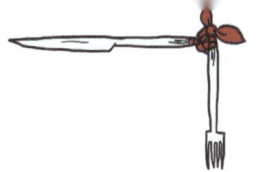

The Place To Get Your Carb Fix

Before the Atkins diet, before Paleo, there was bread. Lots of it.

A Passion for Pita

Trader Joe's rarely reveals who makes what. Clearly this pita supplier and the Trader had a good relationship to be mentioned in the flyer.

Like many foods Trader Joe's introduced to us, pita bread was definitely not a mainstream American food. One early TJ's shopper recalled the horror of his mom stuffing pita bread with alfalfa sprouts for lunch. No kids tried stealing his sandwiches.

Pita bread at Trader is still a bargain at about $1.49 or so, depending on which size bag you choose. A whole lot easier than making it yourself.

Note to Time Travelers: Don't ask for pita chips! They didn't become a mass-market snack until the 90s.

Pita Bread only 49¢

From the famous ▓▓▓▓▓▓▓ in ▓▓▓▓▓▓▓ we have Pita Bread (sometimes called Bible bread or pocket bread). This whole wheat Pita Bread sells for only 49 cents for a half pound (six Pitas per bag). Compare Pita Bread elsewhere at 89 cents and up.

Raising the Bar on Unsliced Bread

In the old days, pumpernickel was an ethnic bread, found more in specialty European bakeries or international markets. The flyer introduces a better-for-you bread, made with honey instead of sugar.

Is this the best thing since sliced bread? You'd think so after reading the point that you can slice it any thickness you want! Sometimes the best innovations take us back in time.

The Revolution of Raisin' Expectations . . .

RAISIN PUMPERNICKEL

We sell this solid loaf of bread in unsliced form, so you can slice it any thickness you desire for the toaster, and to help preserve the freshness of the raisins. (Trader Joe likes a thick slab, toasted, with a fresh cheese like Ricotta or, best yet, a fresh goat's cheese.)

We call this **Madeleine & Charlotte's** Raisin-Pumpernickel, because Trader Joe's two rapidly aging daughters have been the loaf's biggest aficionadas. It's made from stone ground whole wheat flour, raisins, rye flour, etc. As usual, no preservatives etc. We sell a one pound loaf for only $1.39.

. . . a new baker for Trader Joe's Bread

Last year we introduced **Trader Joe's French Village 8 + 2 Multigrain Bread,** and **Sourdough Rye.** Both were baked by a small baker up in Santa Barbara who has decided to stop shipping to Los Angeles. So we have found a Los Angeles baker of natural breads, who has taken over the Santa Barbara breads, and given us others, described on this page. Naturally, his versions of the Santa Barbara breads will be a little different, but we think they are quite similar. (Both breads are still only 99ᶜ.) All of his breads are free of preservatives, dough conditioners or additives. Honey is used instead of refined sugar as a sweetener.

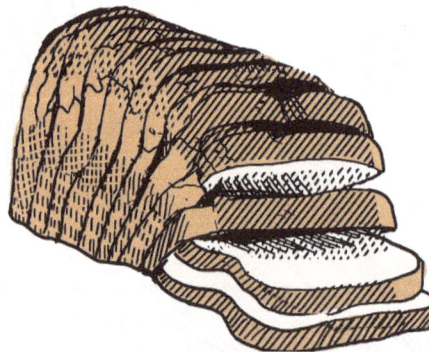

Hot Scoop on the Baker

Notice the charming story about the baker behind Trader Joe's-brand bread. This little anecdote hits home just how small-town the company was, even as a small chain.

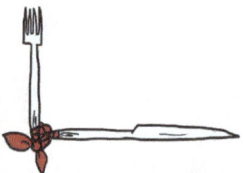

Bread From Steel

The flyer's colorful tale about the Pillars of Hercules bread loaf, baked in a can, is hard to imagine—that is, until you think about the fact that a coffee can isn't so different from a metal bread loaf pan.

Good point, Trader. Why the heck do bakeries still slice bread? I guess it's the best thing since unsliced bread.

In fact the bread-in-a-can has interesting roots in San Francisco's hippie scene, according to author Jonathan Kauffman. "The Diggers—a radical-theatrical group of Haight Ashbury hippie activists—began baking whole-wheat bread in 1967. They distributed the bread along with their free meals in the Panhandle. They shared the recipe far and wide, and it even ended up in *Mother Earth News.*"[11]

PILLARS OF HERCULES:
Whole Grain Bread 99¢

What happens when you bake a loaf of bread in a coffee can? Well, you get a cylindrically shaped loaf. It reminded us of a pillar: that's our story and we're sticking with it. We call the loaves **Pillars of Hercules.**

In the ancient world, the Pillars of Hercules were the Straits of Gibraltar, at the western end of the Mediterranean Sea, marking the end of the known world. In short, the Pillars of Hercules were far out. So is this loaf of bread. It stands alone.

Actually it is a *one and a half pound* loaf of bread, made from stone ground, whole wheat flour, honey, rolled oats, cracked wheat, yeast, gluten, sea salt and soy oil. No preservatives, etc. That's a lot of bread for 99 cents! Of course, it is unsliced, so it can maintain its standing in the community.

In recognition of the mythological origins of this bread, the label's illustration is from an ancient Greek vase. The label may bring bread-selling into the 21st century (A.D.).

---

[11] Kaufmann, Jonathan, "Diggers fed the masses with 'free' as their mantra", *San Francisco Chronicle*, http://www.sfchronicle.com/entertainment/amp/Diggers-fed-the-masses-with-free-as-their-10987583.php and *Hippie Food: How Back-to-the-Landers, Longhairs, and Revolutionaries Changed the Way We Eat* http://amzn.to/2lUQqSV

A Better Muffin Mix

In the early 80s, mixes from Betty Crocker and Duncan Hines still ruled the shelves. The mark of a health-conscious household was a jar of Wheat Germ in the pantry. The fibrous fluffy tan bits resembled saw dust and claimed to deliver all sorts of health benefits.

Trader Joe's could have easily made a less healthy version of a bran muffin mix at a lower cost. Instead they found a muffin mix similar to a recipe you could make at home. And their move to exclude sweetener so more people could buy the mix? Brilliant.

While breakfast cereal companies cranked out colorful jingles to go with their colorful cereals, Trader Joe's was schooling people on how to increase the "availability of protein." This was the beginning of nutritional awareness, that's still taking baby steps even today.

The Only Genuine Whole Wheat Bran Muffin Mix . . .

With the tremendous surge of interest in high-fiber diets, bran muffins have enjoyed a special popularity in the last five years.

The problem is that all of the so-called whole wheat muffin mixes are diluted with white flour, corn starch, etc. Reason: it is really hard to make a genuine whole wheat bran muffin stick together.

Back in Illinois, however, we found a manufacturer who has a bran muffin mix which is not only genuine, but which makes a terrific muffin. Its ingredients are whole wheat flour, wheat bran, yogurt solids, baking soda, soy powder, and flavorings. The presence of the soy, of course, increases the availability of protein in the wheat.

There is no sweetener in the mix, so you can make sugar-free muffins if you wish. Our preference, however, is to add a little honey for flavor, and this alternative is given in the instructions on the package.

We're selling an 8.8 ounce box for 89 cents. Compare so-called whole wheat bran muffin mixes in the health food stores at $.99 to $1.09. This is under our **Madeleine & Charlotte** label (named for Trader Joe's two rapidly aging daughters).

TJ's MAKES MUFFIN HISTORY

A healthier muffin mix comes as no surprise once you know the first "Trader Joe's" brand of food was granola. That was in 1972...back when "granola-eating hippie" was a bit of a slur.[12]

Buns of Whole Grain

How fascinating that a regional grocery chain got their special buns on a major airline like TWA. That's what can happen when people really love your buns!

Nowadays, airlines scour food trade shows for finds like this. Not TWA though. They are long out of business, although the name may ring a bell. The fictional Don Draper flew TWA on *Mad Men*, years before the non-fiction Attila the Buns made an appearance on the airline.

.rader Joe Exclusive
Attila the Bun:
Whole Grain Buns 99¢

These barbarous buns are made from stone-ground whole wheat flour — and they are oblong in shape, rather than round. They are sold only in restaurants and on TWA — and now at Trader Joe's (an unscheduled carrier).

Covered with sesame seeds, **Attila the Bun** will do excellent service for a steak sandwich, a tuna salad sandwich, etc. — or just plain toasted.

We sell a pound — six buns — for only 99 cents.

"Sack Rome? I thought we'd just brown-bag it!"

[12] TraderJoes.com timeline http://www.traderjoes.com/our-story/timeline

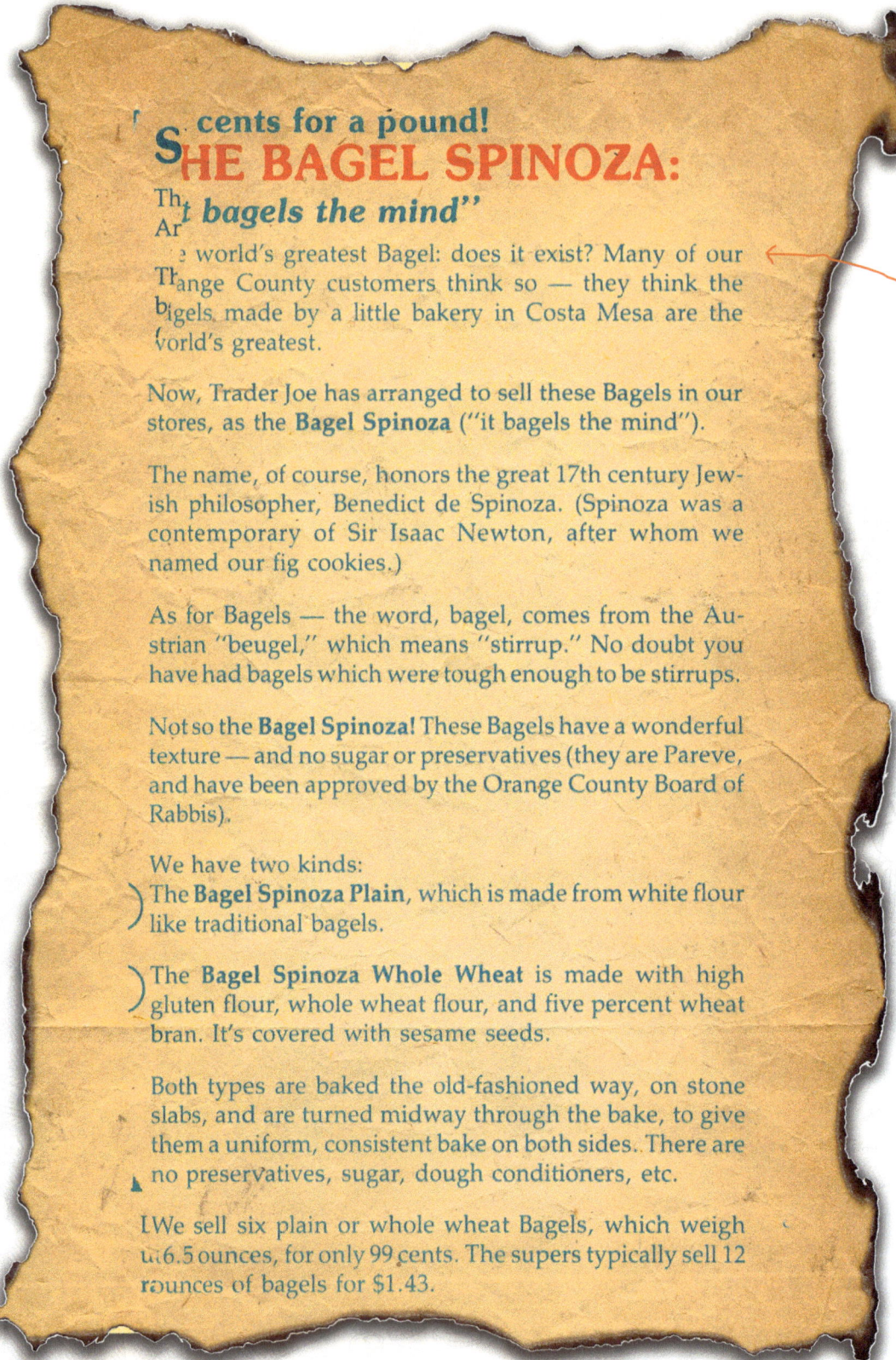

cents for a pound!
SHE BAGEL SPINOZA:

"it bagels the mind"

The world's greatest Bagel: does it exist? Many of our Orange County customers think so — they think the bagels made by a little bakery in Costa Mesa are the world's greatest.

Now, Trader Joe has arranged to sell these Bagels in our stores, as the **Bagel Spinoza** ("it bagels the mind").

The name, of course, honors the great 17th century Jewish philosopher, Benedict de Spinoza. (Spinoza was a contemporary of Sir Isaac Newton, after whom we named our fig cookies.)

As for Bagels — the word, bagel, comes from the Austrian "beugel," which means "stirrup." No doubt you have had bagels which were tough enough to be stirrups.

Not so the **Bagel Spinoza!** These Bagels have a wonderful texture — and no sugar or preservatives (they are Pareve, and have been approved by the Orange County Board of Rabbis).

We have two kinds:
) The **Bagel Spinoza Plain**, which is made from white flour like traditional bagels.

) The **Bagel Spinoza Whole Wheat** is made with high gluten flour, whole wheat flour, and five percent wheat bran. It's covered with sesame seeds.

Both types are baked the old-fashioned way, on stone slabs, and are turned midway through the bake, to give them a uniform, consistent bake on both sides. There are no preservatives, sugar, dough conditioners, etc.

LWe sell six plain or whole wheat Bagels, which weigh u 6.5 ounces, for only 99 cents. The supers typically sell 12 r ounces of bagels for $1.43.

Hooray for Better Bagels

The bagel scene in Southern California at the time of this flyer was nothing short of dry. Noah's, Einstein, and all those nationwide chains had yet to come onto the scene. You could buy Lender's Bagels at the supermarket or track down the occasional deli or local bagel shop— like the Costa Mesa bagelry that brought TJ's The Bagel Spinoza.

Am I the only one who wants to time travel for prices like six stone-slab-baked bagels for $.99? No wonder Dad kept insisting that New York bagels should cost $.25 each.

Bags of six bagels today go for around $3, with all kinds of flavor choices. It takes a lot of self-discipline to skip that bagel shelf.

FRESH!

Nuts & Fruits

All Our Faves, Minus One

History 101... Through Cashews

Readers of the flyer were treated to a mini-international affairs and economics lesson, with cashews as the example. This story shows how buying in bulk ties in to low prices. (The way TJ's locked in that low, low price is similar to what air-lines sometimes do when gas prices sink.) Cashew fans know that the nuts now cost around $6-8 per pound.

Based on what you've read, can you figure out why might prices be higher compared to 1982?

CASHEW PIECES $1.49 Pound

In October we broke the price of Cashew Pieces to $2.19. In November we broke the price again, to $1.69. And now we can break it to $1.49.

What happened? In November, the cashew market collapsed, because the Russians stopped their normal support of their African allies, whose principal crop is cashews. (Now, we can guess that the Russians needed the money for the Poland incident.)

Prices plunged into December — and our buyer, Doug Rauch, locked up 57,000 pounds at very low costs. Then, the West Germans entered the market in force — and cashews have been rising ever since.

Trader Joe, however, wound up with those 57,000 pounds — which we are now selling for only $1.49.

Take note of the cashew buyer's name, Doug Rauch. You'll read more about him on page 67.

A Pecan Bonanza

Pecan pie is an American tradition. But who ever hears of specific pecan varieties? We did then, thanks to Trader Joe's. With the volume of pecans that TJ's sells now, they might have a hard time naming the variety. That variety could change quite frequently, based on weather and harvest sizes.

Nuts For Low Prices

Since the time of this flyer, the price of Trader Joe's fancy mixed nuts has doubled. Now the TJ's mixed nuts price is similar to what supermarket prices were 35 years ago!

The flyer compares the nuts' quality and price to the major nut brand. How could a bargain-hunting nut lover resist?

PECANS $2.99 Pound

Fresh from the 1981 harvest, we have raw·(unroasted) Pecan Halves for only $2.99 per pound.

These Pecans are from the Schley species, grown in New Mexico, and are fancy grade. We have 10 tons at this special price.

Elsewhere, you' pay $4.59 to $7.25 per pound.

"Don't think that soft sell will get far with me, Trader Joe!"

No peanuts!
FANCY MIXED NUTS $2.99 lb.

Trader Joe hereby breaks the price of Fancy Mixed Nuts. We're selling them for only $2.99 per pound — and you have your choice of roasted/salted or raw.

Our rich mix consists of Pecan Halves, Whole Nonpareil Almonds, Whole Cashews, and Walnut Halves — in approximately equal amounts. (No peanuts.)

You might compare **Planter's** in the supers at the equivalent of $6.12 to $6.47 per pound.

Hey, Where Are the Almonds?

Gasp! A flyer that doesn't feature this staple? Maybe almonds were just too basic. They were definitely not a big deal like they are today, a cure-all diet food, with choices of pack sizes and exotic flavors.

A major producer of snacking almonds from California (which supplies most of the world crop) is a grower co-operative. Nut lovers know the name: Blue Diamond. In the early 80s, Blue Diamond was producing almonds in varieties including Smokehouse, Barbeque, Cheese, Green Onion, Onion-Garlic, Roasted Salted, and Unsalted Dry Roasted. Pretty all-American, eh?

The ethnic flavor trend we see nowadays of Salsa-this and Sriracha-that was decades away. Thanks to our appetite for almonds, the California crop quadrupled between 1970 and 2000.

Please note: Should you find yourself time traveling to 1982, don't request almond milk. This drink may be as ancient as almond trees, but it didn't take off as a mainstream drink in America until years later.

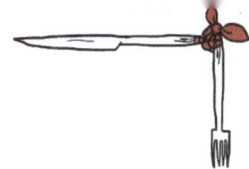

A College Education in Apricots

Apricot lovers may find themselves drooling over the flyer's Turkish dried apricots description. But here's a question: California is a major apricot-growing area. The state produces 95 percent of the apricots grown in the U.S. So why not sell American apricots?

The same goes for pistachios and hazelnuts, both of which thrive in Turkey.

Often the answer comes down to which country has the best, cheapest, most plentiful supply in any given year.

APRICOTS FROM TURKEY $2.99 pound

Some of the world's greatest dried apricots come from Turkey.

(The Romans first discovered Apricots in eastern Turkey and Armenia. They named it "Praecocia" — literally, precocious — because of its early, June ripening. "Apricot" is a corruption of Praecocia.)

These are big, whole apricots which have been "slit pitted". That means a small slit was made in the side of each 'cot, and the pit removed — leaving the appearance of the fruit almost undisturbed. They have been lightly sulfured to preserve their color.

We have only 15,000 pounds of these beauties (Doug Rauch, our buyer of dried fruit, thinks these are some of the best Turkish dried apricots he has ever seen). At $2.99 they're a bargain — Turkish Apricots usually sell for $4.29 to $5.49 per pound.

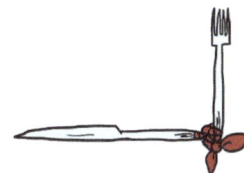

FIGS
RADICALLY REDUCED

For some reason, ███████ offered us 12,000 packages of figs at a radically reduced cost (down about a third). As a result we can sell these half-pound packages for only 99 cents. Compare figs in the supers at $1.39 to $1.59.

These are extra fancy Calimyrna figs, fresh from the 1981 harvest.

Good News for Fig Lovers

This has got to be one of the best flyer stories ever—how "for some reason" this supplier offered TJ's a load of California figs.

And so the fig-loving public got their hands on this special batch of bargain-priced California figs.

Welcome to Pescatarian Paradise

A Salmon Story

Out of all the rare foods Trader Joe's landed, this Oncorhynchus tshawytscha (otherwise known as King salmon, or Chinook salmon) was a real score.

This Food of the Grizzly bear must have been a welcome antidote for college students, sick of long nights of pilchard-eating (more on this on page 30). You rarely find canned Chinook Salmon these days for less than $15 or so a can. We've got to send the Trader fishing for more.

Another Shipment!
The RARE CHINOOK SALMON

Last October a customer came into our Costa Mesa store and told Tom Hetzel, our manager, that **Trader Joe's Chinook** was the best canned salmon he had ever eaten. This reaction was typical, and we sold out the entire shipment in four weeks.

Since then, we have been combing the Pacific Northwest for more Chinook. It's hard to find, because almost all Chinook is sold fresh or smoked, because of its high quality.

We were lucky, though, and found another 270 cases. We're selling it at the same low price — $1.49 per 7.75 ounce can. Compare ordinary red salmon in the supers at $1.99-$2.37.

Fresh Pack Alaska Pink Salmon

Fresh from the 1981 catch, we have **Trader Joe's Alaska Pink Salmon.**

How do we buy our pink salmon? We're small enough that we can buy our pink salmon lot by lot. We do this by blind-tasting samples from each lot submitted by the packers — each lot is relatively small (750 cases). Salmon does vary tremendously from lot to lot — for an explanation of this we suggest you read **Consumer Reports** of May, 1981.

We're selling a "tall" can (15.75 ounces) for only $1.99. Compare at $2.37 to $2.49 in most supers.

A Fish Called Pilchard?

Pilchard: a small, oily fish. The word "pilchard" sounds small and oily. Turns out they're young sardines. The flyer cleverly compares this small, oily fish to a familiar food. Shoppers were lured to try something new and love it (or not).

Today Trader Joe's brings us an array of tinned fish that can turn any zombie apocalypse stash into a gourmet party.

On a recent visit, I counted herring, sardines (smoked, in water, and in olive oil), mackerel, smoked oysters, anchovy fillet, smoked trout: But no pilchard!

Is the problem in the supply? Or is it out of style? Perhaps it's the name that didn't catch on: "Not a pilchard sandwich again, Mom!"

Another shipment!
Pilchard: Fish like Tuna for lots less Money

In October we introduced Trader Joe's Pilchard, a fish caught in the South Pacific which closely resembles tuna, even though biologically it belongs to the herring family.

The meat of the Pilchard is lighter than most "green label" or "chunk light" tuna. Because it's not as well known, however, we can sell a seven ounce can for only 69 cents.

The Pilchard introduced in October sold out, but we have just received another 800 cases. It is packed in water.

Tuna Trivia

B.W. (Before Wikipedia), people could rely on the TJ's flyer for essentials like how governments measure tuna and the word origin of "albacore tuna." They not only brought us cheap protein but some really fun cafeteria table talk. Nowadays you can get your hands on albacore tuna for around $1.69 at Trader.

"Canadian Albacore" —

"Albacore" is a Portuguese word, taken from the Arabic, which means "young camel."

Around the world, however, "Albacore" has come to mean the whitest kind of meat from Tuna fish.

There are many species of Tuna, and several of these yield very white meat. The American Food & Drug Administration has taken the position that only one of these species, *Thunus alalungus*, is Albacore. This is the only Tuna which can be labeled "Albacore;" it is the only Tuna which can be labeled "white meat tuna" — even when its meat isn't very white!

he Rare Big Eye Tuna 99¢

Other governments, however, have taken the more logical position that "white meat" tuna should be judged by a spectroscope, not by the species of fish involved.

In Canada, some "white meat" or "Albacore" tuna comes from a rare species, *Parathunnus mebachi*, commonly known as Big Eye Tuna. That's because much of its meat can pass the spectroscopic standard the Canadians have established, as to what is "white" tuna.

Because of the American bureaucratic glitch, we can buy Big Eye Tuna for a lot less than *Thunnus alalunga*. It's just that we have to label it "chunk light." We can't call it "Albacore" or "white meat."

We **can**, however, sell Big Eye Tuna for only 99¢ in 6.5 ounce cans at a time when bureaucratic-Albacore sells for $1.35 to $1.50 in the supers. We think you'll agree that **Trader Joe's Big Eye Tuna** swims in the same school as Albacore. It's packed in water.

New Twists On Old Favorites

It's Only Natural

Revolutionary Peanut Butter

Once upon a time, we had only a choice of natural peanut butter or not-so-natural peanut butter.

Leave it to Trader Joe's to dish out the backstory on their pioneering pure pea-nutty goodness. The flyer's details are almost as juicy as the $.99 per pound price. Juicier still is the comparison to a big-time peanut butter brand.

In 1982, folks in Trader-less territory had to trek to a health food store—like Whole Foods' single store in Austin, Texas—to get a peanut butter made simply from ground peanuts and salt.

TJ insiders know that now we can choose from butters made from different kinds of peanuts, with flax seeds added, organic or not. That's more than the old days but still fewer than what most supermarkets carry. Less choice is one thing we love about TJ's! (See p. 66)

NATURAL PEANUT BUTTER: 99¢ Pound!

Fresh from the 1981 harvest, we have 100% natural peanut butter for only 99 cents per pound. This is the lowest price in the United States, for peanut butter with no additives, hydrogenated oils, sugar, etc. etc.

Produced by a religious community in the Northwest, we have both creamy and crunchy grinds — the creamy is unsalted; the crunchy is salted.

This peanut butter is so fresh, and unstabilized, that it should be refrigerated after opening. We can sell this in ounce plastic tubs at 93¢ which is 99¢ per pound, under the Natural Food Store label.

Compare **Laura Scudder** in the supers at $1.71-1.75.

Before Vegan Culture

Carpe meatless chili! Once again, the flyer's detailed product description makes the most die-hard meat lover crave this vegetarian chili made with fresh ingredients. And you can bet this was the first time lots of people had heard of Tamari.

The Latin language and references to eating dogs (canis) are not as common these days in TJ's flyers, for obvious reasons. While no one ever called TJ's politically correct, they clearly would prefer to avoid rumors that Fire God Chili is made with man's best friend. This random ramble is yet another peek into Trader Joe's genuine love of food…and their quirky humor.

VEGETARIAN CHILI

Boy, if you want to get in an argument, just claim you have "authentic" chili. 10,000 backyard chefs wil at your throat.

For those of you who believe that chili without beef a chili — may we gently point out that beef is not nativ North America, and that the ancient civilizations of M ico had been cooking dishes much like "chili" for 10, years (at least) before Cortez showed up. (If you wan *authentic* meat for chili — How Much is that *Canis* in Window?)

So here we have **Trader José's Fire God** Vegetarian C No animal products whatsoever (which, speaking ancient civilizations, qualifies it as **Pareve** for the Jev community).

It tastes pretty good. The protein in the kidney bear made more "available" by the addition of protein f soy beans — this is texturized vegetable protein, wl has the texture of meat. Only fresh onions are used dehydrated). There's no modified food starch, su preservatives, etc. There is a small amount of honey, a small amount of Tamari soy sauce.

The product is sold frozen in plastic tubs which hold pound. **Trader José's Fire God Chili** is only $1.2! compare similar products elsewhere at $1.59 to $1,!

Real Men Heat Quiche

The gang at TJ's again led the curve with a better-for-you quiche, free of preservatives and sugar, and made with whole wheat flour. How could such a good quiche be so darn cheap? The flyer explains Quiche Economics, removing any doubt about the quiches' quality.

But wait! Where there's a good story, there's good drama. A humorous book called *Real Men Don't Eat Quiche (a guidebook to all that is Truly Masculine)* came out in April, 1982—one month after Trader Joe's declared this Health Food Quiche a big seller.

We will never know if quiche sales went down yet as book sales went up. Lucky for TJ's, the book did not pooh-pooh "real men" *buying* quiche (just *making* quiche).

Health Food Quiche: Save 70¢

Last year we introduced two "health food" Quiches under our label: **Trader Joe's French Village Quiche Lorraine,** and **Spinach Quiche.** Each sold for $3.69.

Our volume has been so great, however, that the woman who bakes these for us has cut our cost — and we're passing the savings on to you. Effective at once, therefore, we're selling them for only $2.99, per 18 ounce Quiche.

Both are made with 100% whole wheat flour, no sugar, no preservatives, no lard or hydrogenated oils, etc.

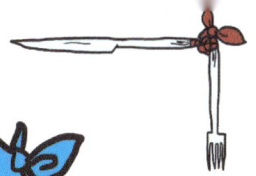

Pie. That's it.

Really? Just pie?

Was Trader Joe's that health conscious? You've got to assume there were more desserts than the tasty-sounding pies featured in this flyer.

As a TJ's fan, you know today's array of endless sweets make every shopping trip an exercise in resistance.

How much do we love TJ's desserts? Customers have been known to start online petitions to bring back discontinued sweets. (Pre-Internet, sugar-deprived customers must have turned to letter-writing campaigns, pitchforks, and protests.)

. across the river and into the freeze . . .

HAND MADE BOYSENBERRY PIE

From the small baker who supplies our apple pie, now we have Boysenberry pie. The pies are made from fresh-frozen, whole Boysenberries, from the 1981 harvest. The crust is made without lard, or preservatives. There is no artificial flavoring or coloring, in either crust or filling.

We sell a 32 ounce pie for only $3.99.

A World of Drinks

TJ's Quenched
Our Thirst For
Adventurous Drinks

California Wine Pioneers

Wine With Dinner - How European

In the early 80s, few Americans popped open a bottle of wine to wind down in the evening. There weren't all of those greeting cards, t-shirts, and medical studies about the joys and benefits of wine. Table wines costing $3 a bottle or less were not very common. Quite the opposite. A $3 wine was generally pretty bad, usually hidden in a brown paper bag for clandestine sipping.

Imports made up around 25% of wines consumed in the early 80s.[13]

5000 Cases Sold
TIPO CHIANTI 99¢

Last fall we introduced **Tipo** Chianti, a California "ch[ian]ti" remarkably like the real stuff from Italy. We have [sold] **five thousand cases,** but since we had to buy 7800 c[ases] to get this incredibly low price, we still have plenty

This wine has gotten raves from hundreds of custom[ers] — one church group bought 400 cases! At 99 cents it is [the] best bargain in red wine in Los Angeles.

An American Chianti!

Italian Chianti was one of the more popular cheap wines. You know, the wine with the familiar round bottom, wrapped in straw. It is famously seen on red-checked tablecloths in Italian-themed movies. An American Chianti was a real innovation. Clearly this L.A. church agreed. (Stocking up for communion services!?)

Europeans have a long tradition of drinking very good and very cheap wine with meals. They call it "table wine." (So when you see *vin de table* in France, you'll know it means just good enough to drink with a meal on a not-so-special occasion.)

---

[13] D. Heien and P. Martin, "California's wine industry enters new era," *University of California, Davis,* http://ucce.ucdavis.edu/files/repositoryfiles/ca5703p71-70204.pdf

Even in the 1960s, Trader Joe's was a top seller of California wines and was among the first to give unknown California wines a chance.

This was a big deal. Although Californians had been making wine since their immigrant ancestors had come to California decades earlier (some in the 1800s), California wine was only a blip on the radar of the "good wine" world—much as it was with cheese.

Fresh from the '81 Harvest
WHITE ZINFANDEL $1.99

Fresh from the 1981 harvest, here is "white" Zinfandel. Trader Joe's 1981 North Coast Counties White Zinfandel was produced by the same winery that produced our 1979 White Zin, and it has the same, delicate pink color—the result of separating the juice from the black-skinned grapes as soon as the grapes were crushed. It is a terch drier than the 1980.

(Bureaucratic note: Our White Zinfandel originally was called "Aurora", in deference to the pink Goddess of the Dawn. Night Must Fall, however, the Federal authorities decreed: Aurora is also the name of a grape grown in New York. Although our wine is clearly labelled "White Zinfandel", it was feared that some customers would think it was made from Aurora grapes. If it was made from Aurora grapes, we would be fearful, too.)

European wines were *it*. You didn't really see much in the way of wines from Australia, Chile or the various countries whose wines we enjoy today.

Things changed in 1976, at the so-called Judgment of Paris wine competition. Here, at this blind wine tasting, California proved its wines to be on par with the world's best.[14]

Trader Joe's was poised for success, given their pioneering wine connections. "One of the ways we built this business was to bring in obscure wineries, the antithesis of Gallo, and offer them to the public..." founder Joe Coulombe told the *Los Angeles Times*.[15]

---

[14] The book *The Judgment of Paris* and movie *Bottle Shock*, about this competition, will have you on the edge of your seat, even if you're not really into wine.
[15] "Buyer for Trader Joe's stores helped popularize wine," *Los Angeles Times*, July 22, 2008
http://articles.latimes.com/2008/jul/22/local/me-berning22

The Pioneer Buyer Behind the Wines

The store's wine buyer Robert Berning innovated in "not just the buying of the wines, but the logistics: our ability to distribute the wines to our stores because conventional wholesalers were not going to do that for us."[16]

Stocking rare and interesting wines was a win for the wineries and a win for TJ's. The store drew in customers the same way it did with foods you couldn't find elsewhere. Needless to say, amazing wines at bargain prices was (and is!) a win for shoppers.

Way Before Two Buck Chuck

Would $1.99 Charles Shaw wines have taken off if $.99 Chianti had been around? We'll never know. We do know that the wine we call "Two Buck Chuck" sold about 600 million bottles in its first 10 years.[17]

980 CHARDONNAY $2.69

From a major winery in Sonoma County, we have Trader Joe's 1980 Northern California Chardonnay. The grapes come predominantly from Sonoma, San Luis Obispo, Santa Barbara, and Monterey Counties. The result of this blend is a fresh, dry Chardonnay with quite a bit of varietal character. It will develop more complexity with a few months of bottle age. At 2.69 this is good value.

---

[16] "Buyer for Trader Joe's stores helped popularize wine," *Los Angeles Times*, July 22, 2008 http://articles.latimes.com/2008/jul/22/local/me-berning22

[17] TraderJoes.com http://www.traderjoes.com/fearless-flyer/article/433

Just like today, they used the newsletter to educate and entice customers to come in and try some new wines.

Perhaps Napa Valley Chenin Blanc—whose maker the flyer slyly avoids telling us—was advertised alongside French Chardonnay to give it enough panache so we'd give it a try. Even back in 1982, $3.49 for 1.5 liters wasn't bad. And if the wine was bad, Julia Child would surely have endorsed using it in a soup or sauce.

Why Pay $8.50?
KORBEL SPARKLING BURGUNDY $3.49

Korbel, the famous producer of California champagne, produces several kinds of sparkling wine. One of these is **Korbel Rouge**, a rich sparkling burgundy. Suggested retail on **Korbel Rouge** is $8.50.

Korbel, however, has decided to discontinue the label (we suspect because the public prefers to buy pink sparkling wine that is called "Blanc de Noirs"). They had 1800 cases of **Korbel Rouge** left at the winery. We bought it all — and we're selling it for only $3.49. This is a terrific wine to serve with steak.

French Chardonnay $2.89

Here's another in the series of white Burgundies which we can sell for only $2.89: 1980 Pinot Chardonnay Macon **Robert Ledoux**. It's a fresh, clean, acid wine. We have 1000 cases.

Napa Valley CHENIN BLANC 1.5 Liter $3.49

Here's a good, big bottle of wine for parties. This is a light, mildly sweet, Chenin Blanc, made 100% from grapes grown in the Napa Valley. It was produced by a winery (name withheld) in the famous wine village of Rutherford, in the heart of the Valley, and labelled under the **Napa Wine Co.** brand. We have 2500 cases of 1.5 Liter bottles (cork finish) at only $3.49.

Trader Joe's
SONOMA BRUT CHAMPAGNE $5.99

This wine, like most of our private label wine, has a "real" name. We cannot disclose the brand, but it sells for $12.00 per bottle in most stores. We sell it for $5.99.

In December, one of the prominent wine shops in Los Angeles got hold of this wine, under its "real" name, and promoted it for $9.00. They called it "superb".

Of course, we agree. Trader Joe thinks it is the finest wine we have issued under our name. And he ordered another thousand cases from the winery, just to put his money where his mouth is.

"There! What more proof do you need that Trader Joe put his money where his mouth is?"

Champagne From California?

The elegantly simple name Trader Joe's Sonoma Brut Champagne took me by surprise.

Doesn't a sparkling wine have to be from the Champagne region of France to be called Champagne?

Not as of 1980. The U.S. Food & Drug Administration (FDA) describes the Court ruling after a lawsuit on this very subject: "A wine having substantially the same qualities as French champagne and produced substantially in the same way, originating in California, should not be held

A dry Trader Joe's? It may be hard for some customers to imagine, but some laws around the country still ban grocery stores like TJ's from selling alcoholic beverages.

to be misbranded if labeled 'California 'Champagne'."[17] There you have it.

Now we wonder: Was this TJ Champagne from Korbel, whose Sparkling Burgundy they were selling? Or perhaps Gloria Ferrer, who still makes a highly praised Sonoma Brut? Some questions are better left unanswered. The important thing is there's no shortage of superb sparkling wines from around the world (at Trader Joe's that are allowed to sell alcohol, that is).

THE BEST BEAUJOLAIS

Georges DuBoeuf (rhymes with woof) is one of the best known producers of Beaujolais in France.

Like other French winemakers, however, **DuBoeuf** became interested in California. In 1980 **DuBoeuf** took grapes grown in Northern California, and had them vinified at the famous **Jordan** winery by Tom Jordan. **DuBoeuf** used a blend of 90% Gamay Beaujolais and 10% Petit Syrah grapes.

The result is a voluptuous Beaujolais, full of the fruit that you would expect in real Beaujolais from a village like Fleurie.

IN CALIFORNIA $1.99

The wine was released to sell at about $5.00 per bottle **DuBoeuf** had a problem, however. As honest Frenchmen, they refused to call the wine "Gamay Beaujolais." Instead, they labeled it "1980 North Coast Red Table Wine." Although the price was fair, the public did not see through the label.

So that's how we were able to buy all 1500 cases, and sell this classic wine for only $1.99. We think it's the best Beaujolais style wine produced in California in the last two years. And with prices of French Beaujolais sky-high right now, because of a series of mediocre harvests, we think it's the best bargain in this style of wine in the world.

---

[17] CPG Sec. 510.300 Unfermented Beverages - Use of Word "Champagne" http://www.fda.gov/ICECI/Compliance-Manuals/CompliancePolicyGuidanceManual/ucm074429.htm

At Home With French Wine Bargains

How do you say "$1.49 Charles" in French?

FRENCH COUNTRY WINE — RED AND WHITE $1.49

Here's an unusual French wine: it's labeled "Vin de Pays" — "Country Wine" — but the place of origin has been specified on the label. Usually "Vin de Pays" doesn't do this.

"I don't care where it was grown, Trader Joe — as long as it was not beyond the boundaries of good taste!"

The wine was grown in the "Bouches du Rhone" — the mouth of the Rhone River, where it empties into the Mediterranean Sea. This area is not known for great wines — the area should not be confused with the noble "Cotes du Rhone," 100 miles to the north.

This "Bouches du Rhone", however, is respectable value — both the white and the red. The White has plenty of acid; the Red does resemble the reds of the Cotes du Rhone.

We have these wines under the **Sommeliere** brand, a total of 1600 cases, red and white, in regular bottles and 1.5 liter bottles. Good value at $1.49 ($2.98 for the 1.5 liter).

BIG COTES du RHONE $2.99

1976 Cotes du Rhone Villages Reserve des Chapelains $2.99/one hour air at least! This is a great big wine. 1976 was a fine year in the Rhone, and this wine, produced by the well known house of Salavert, has a big structure. It takes all that air to develop its potential. We have 700 cases.

FRENCH WINES
from the famous
ROLAND THEVENIN $1.99

Roland Thevenin (pronounced Tevv-uh-nanh) is one of the best known producers of fine Burgundian wines, which sell for very high prices. Thevenin, however, has now introduced some "vin de table" which we can sell for only $1.99.

Roland Thevenin Rouge $1.99 is overtly Burgundian in character — a blend of the premier grapes of southern Burgundy (Gamay) and Northern Burgundy (Pinot Noir). Soft, full flavored, dry red wine. We have 700 cases.

Roland Thevenin Blanc $1.99 Dry, sound white wine. We are told it has some of the press juice from his famous chardonnay vines, but of course we have no direct knowledge of this, and offer it just as a very good value in white wine. 700 cases.

On Through German Wine Country

From the Greatest German Vineyard, No Less!

The topic of German wines is a good time to bring up a little known fact about TJ's: For most of its life, a German fellow, Theo Albrecht, owned Trader Joe's. Founder Joe Coulombe sold his baby to Albrecht in 1979.

Perhaps this is how TJ's got access to such great German wine knowledge along with "QbA wein."

Most of the German wines in this sale are "Qba," which is a trade abbreviation for Qualitatswein. What's that?

It means "quality" wine in German — distinguishing it from "Tafelwein" or table wine. All Qba's must be tested by the government, and are assigned official quality-control numbers (Amtliche prufnummer).

As a practical matter, the Qba's fall between the low-class Tafelweins, and the "pradikat" or "pedigree" wines — the Kabinetts, Spatlesen, Auslesen, etc.

Thanks Trader Joe's! We will thank you the next time we're drinking Tafelwein.

45

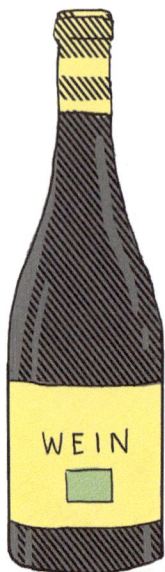

WINES FROM THE MOSEL

1977 Graacher Himmelreich Riesling Qba **Weingut Meyerhof** $1.99   Estate bottled. Graach (pronounced Grack) is just across from Bernkastel. Himmelreich is its best known vineyard. The wine is mildly sweet. 185 cases.

1977 Graacher Himmelreich Riesling Qba **Reichsgraf von Kesselstatt** $1.99   Estate bottled. Although the label reads the same as the first wine, this one is utterly different. Quite dry. 200 cases.

1977 Graacher Josephshofer Riesling Qba **von Kesselstatt** $2.49   Josephshof is a famous single vineyard which belongs exclusively to the von Kesselstatt family. Dry, pungent Riesling. 200 cases.

1977 Scharzhofberger Riesling Qba **Weingut von Hovel** $2.89   Estate bottled. Scharzhofberg is accepted by the world as the greatest vineyard in the Saar; Trader Joe thinks it's the greatest vineyard in Germany! This particular wine is a truly great wine, one of the best *dry* German wines we have tasted. Excellent balance and body. Hooray! 160 cases.

1977 Ockfener Bockstein Qba **Duenweg** $1.99   Ockfen is one of the finest villages in the Saar; Bockstein is considered its leading vineyard. 300 cases.

Trader Joe Lowers the Boom on German Wine Prices!
7000 Cases on Sale

This is the greatest sale of German wines we have had in four years. A combination of a weak Deutschemark, and high American interest rates, forced a major importer of German wines to close out its inventory of 1977 vintage wines. Almost all of the wines are **Frank Schoonmaker** selections; generally we have been pleased with the selections made by Mr. Schoonmaker's successors (the late, great Frank Schoonmaker died in 1976.)

In addition to the wines shown here, we have many other wines in this sale, whose individual quantities were too small to be shown.

This was Germany's currency before the Euro!

German wines may not have the lure of French and Italian, but after reading these blurbs, you'd have had a hard time resisting them.

When buying wine at Trader Joe's, you will very likely find a staffer who's a wine geek. They'll happily recommend bottles to your liking and maybe even help you pronounce "Wachenheimer Bischofsgarten Riesling."

"That's a hell of a way to lower the boom!"

1977 came in the shadow of 1976, which, because of profound drought, was the best year in Germany in many decades. As a result, the 77er's tended to be over-looked, just as the great '62 Bordeaux wines were over-looked, because of '61. All of the 77er's offered here however, are fine wines (in the classic sense), and all of them can spend more years in the bottle.

WINES FROM THE RHINEPFALZ

1977 Wachenheimer Bischofsgarten Riesling Qba **Dr. Burklin-Wolf** $1.99   Estate bottled. Wachenheim is one of the top villages in the Pfalz; Bischofsgarten one of its less known vineyards. The wine is clean, light bodied and relatively dry. 290 cases. Burklin-Wolf is one of the most celebrated producers of the Pfalz.

1977 Wachenheimer Mariengarten Riesling Qba **Dr. Burklin-Wolf** $1.99. Somewhat drier, more pungent wine. 190 cases.

Drinking Spanish Style

No Need For a Eurail Pass

Upping the Brandy Game

Chances are a sentence like "best buy in brandy to be found in Los Angeles" propelled my Dad from his chair and into the car to grab that bottle of "José Primero," just one of Trader Joe's charming variations on the "Joe" name.

Leave it to TJ's to can make a critique sound delicious: Who knew that bad brandy had a banana-oil character? What is banana oil? When will Trader Joe's carry some? I want it for my ice cream.

TEN YEAR OLD SPANISH BRANDY $3.99

This is probably the best buy in brandy to be found in Los Angeles.

The brandy was grown in Spain, and aged for ten years before being bottled. It is a dry brandy, rather resembling Cognac with a finish of unsweetened chocolate. What we like best is the absence of the banana-oil character of cheap California brandy; or the harshness of cheap European brandy.

We're selling this under our **José Primero** label for only $3.99.

Sherry Baby

Are you hip to sherry? This historic Spanish wine is fortified, usually, with brandy. This clever technique preserves the wine, giving it a longer shelf life.

Sherry may seem like an obscure drink. In fact, it has played a major role in American cocktail history. For inspiration to grab a bottle (maybe not for $1.49), take a look at Saveur Magazine's online article: *How an Old Sherry Drink Defined an Era of American History.*[18]

Trivia: Sherry, called *Jerez* in Spanish, is made from grapes even though it sounds like "cherry." (*Cereza* is the word for cherries in Spanish, a little lesson to aid your alcohol requests when in Spain or at Trader Joe's.)

[18] Search for the article title on Saveur.com. or, for literature buffs, chew on Charles Dickens' The Life and Adventures of Martin Chuzzlewit

$3.99.

From Spain . . .
"SHERRY" $1.49

"Sherry" wine is produced in southern Spain around a town called Jerez de la Frontera ("Sherry" is an English corruption of the word, Jerez). The boundaries of the region which produces Sherry have drifted over the centuries.

Under present bureaucratic definitions, there is the official "Sherry" region, around Jerez de la Frontera; another region which officially produces "Montilla" wine; and still other regions nearby, all of which produce wines which resemble Sherry and Montilla, but which cannot use those names.

One of these satellite regions, about 15 miles north of Jerez de la Frontera, is Arcos de la Frontera.

From Arcos de la Frontera we have **La Peña** Cream, which we are selling for only $1.49. It is quite similar to cream sherry, and has the advantage of only 16% alcohol, which gives it a lightness not always found in Spanish sherry, and never found in California "sherry." (It seems crazy to worry about differences of 15 miles within Spain, when California baldly mis-uses the term, sherry, on millions of cases of wine each year.)

We have 1600 cases of **La Peña.**

"In California, you can call it Sherry, if it's grown any place north of Tijuana de la Frontera!"

49

Before the Big Craft Beer Thing

Exotic Imported Beer!

Yesssss. $1.99 divided by six = ***really cheap***. Even though you could get 12 packs of Hamm's beer for this price back then, $1.99 for a trip to Italy (via a six-pack) was a real bargain. When in Rome, you can still treat yourself to Birra Raffo and flash back to reading this very flyer.

Beer From Italy $1.99 for 6

Anyone who has visited Italy knows that the beer there is quite good. Birra **Raffo**, brewed in Rome, has that authentic Italian flavor. Only 2500 cases at this bargain price.

$$(3 \times (\$1.50)_{WINE})$$
$$+ (2 \times (\$3.99)_{CHEESE})$$
$$+$$

Coffee For the People

Hang Out In Cafes? Not So Much

There Was a Time Before Starbucks Roamed the Earth

In 1982, requesting a "double flat white latte with caramel syrup" would have drawn blank looks, like a scene from *Back to the Future*. Supermarkets sold ground coffee in plastic-lidded tins, brands like Yuban®[19] , Sanka®, Folgers® and Maxwell House®. Instant coffees like Nescafé®, which dissolve in water, came in jars.

Most coffee drinkers sipped much weaker brews than what you find in cafes today. Not until 1984 did Starbucks serve its first Caffe Latte in Seattle.

You certainly didn't see whole beans in bags at the typical market. You had to track down a specialty coffee roaster or international market for whole, freshly-roasted beans in person or by mail. (And no, you couldn't order them on Amazon. Remember, the Web didn't come to be for another decade or so.)

WHOLE BEAN COFFEE FROM PERU $2.99

One of the most popular coffees we have ever sold is the Peruvian Excelso. Grown high in the Andes, the coffee is hand picked and dried in the sun before shipment. (Peru is the 19th largest producer of coffee in the world).

We were unable to get Peruvian Excelso last year, but now we're back in stock — and at the same low price of $2.99 per pound. Like all **Trader José** label whole bean coffees, it's packed in nitrogen-flushed cans for freshness.

---

[19] Fans of the movie Airplane: Remember the "Jim never has a second cup of coffee at home" scene? That was a play on a 1972 Yuban TV commercial. Yes, you can see a clip on YouTube.

Coffee and College Go Hand in Hand

College towns throughout California already had their Italian-style cafes, and Peet's Coffee, founded in Berkeley, had a smattering of locations in the San Francisco area.

Yes, there were the coffee equivalents of foodies, like my parents who made "pour over" coffee and Mary Tyler Moore who used a Chemex drip maker on her TV show.

So it's not surprising that early Trader Joe's customers (the ones in "centers of education") would experiment with new coffees and brewing techniques. After all, they needed to stay up late studying then jolt awake. Or maybe they just loved fresh coffee.

I bean loving you for so long, Trader Joe's.

Swiss Decaf Coffee from Belgium

Trader Joe's gave shoppers the full scoop about their supplier, whose name shall remain anonymous. The Swiss Decaf flyer listing is pure genius, akin to the story-like advertising that was popular in the 60s and 70s. Trader Joe's, you even make decaf hard to resist.

The Swiss Process continues to be the most pure and most expensive way to turn caffeinated coffee into decaf, and you can still find decaf using "glacial waters" at Trader Joe's today.

Chapter 2: Crisis in SWISS DECAF COFFEE

In the November **Insider Report**, we told you how the supply of coffee which has been decaffeinated in Switzerland by a steam process, has almost been cut off to America.

Since so many people believe that steam process decaffeination is the only safe process (as opposed to the chemical processes used by **Sanka**, **Brim** and others) this shortage has turned into a crisis.

Just as nature abhors a vacuum, so do suppliers hate to see sales go glimmering. So now we are seeing so-called "European water process" decaf showing up in competitors' stores.

Sure, they use water. As **part** of the decaffeination process. But that doesn't mean they don't use chemicals to extract the caffeine, in other parts of the process.

There is only one, Swiss, decaffeination process which uses nothing but steam, as of this writing. We hope the monopoly will be broken some day. But right now there is only one manufacturer.

Alas, that supplier's name is left to your imagination.

You must appreciate this...

Enjoy how this Trader Joe's writer, obsessed with LA's horrible water spends the entire product description ranting, then uses the slang word "rank" (meaning disgusting) because clearly no other word would do!

Today, Kenya is still known for producing some of the best coffee in the world.

Trader Joe's was so cute and local they could talk about the Los Angeles public broadcasting TV station in the flyer... and customers knew what the heck they're talking about!

HOW TO MAKE COFFEE IN CASABLANCA

You must remember this . . .

CLAUDE RAINS: Why, did you come to Casablanca?
BOGART: To take the waters.
CLAUDE RAINS: There are no waters here. This is a desert.
BOGART: I was misinformed.
— from the 1942 film, "Casablanca"

Anyone who comes to the region of Los Angeles to take the waters must be equally misinformed. If you wonder why your coffee tastes lousy — taste the water. (In that TV commercial — we suspect the reason why the husband wants a second cup is simply that he's away from home, where the water supply is rank.)

We suggest that you try a little empirical experiment. Simply make two pots of coffee — one with tap water; one with bottled water. The results may be illuminating. Here's looking at you, kid!

Highest Grade Whole Bean Coffee from Kenya

The African country of Kenya is famous for its high quality coffee. In Kenya, all coffee is sold only through weekly auctions. Bids are made by grade, and the highest grade of all is "Kenya AA". And that's what Trader Joe is selling here. AA beans are the biggest quality beans grown — what is called an "18 screen". (There is a bigger, 20 screen bean, called Maragogipe, the native word for elephant, but it is not of as high quality as AA. The smallest beans are 13/14 screen.)

This is a snappy coffee, one that jumps right out of the cup. We're selling Kenya AA beans for only $3.69 per pound. Compare elsewhere at $5.29 per pound and up.

Like all of Trader Joe's whole bean coffees, this one is packed in our nitrogen-flushed cans, to preserve freshness.

The Flame Trees of Thika — the distinguished television series on KCET Channel 28 Sunday nights is about the planting of coffee trees in Kenya.

Imported Water For the Masses

You may find this hard to swallow: People did not carry around bottled water like they do today. You could buy fizzy Perrier, from France, or San Pellegrino, from Italy, and America soda water in cans and glass bottles. But there was no endless stream of flavored soda waters—and definitely no vitamin-infused water.

When we wanted distilled or purified water, we would take a gallon jug to the machine at the supermarket and fill it up for $.10.

Were we just less thirsty? Was the world cooler? Did we exercise less? Or maybe the idea of drinking eight cups of water a day hadn't become common wisdom. Just as we slathered cocoa butter to roast our skin to a crispy tan, we drank whenever we felt thirsty.

Fans of the 1992 movie *The Player* may recall our growing water obsession in a satire of Hollywood execs. For each water request, they mention a different brand, including Vitelle,

Why pay 99 cents?
FERRARELLE WATER FROM ITALY 59¢

Ferrarelle was one of the most famous springs of the ancient world. Located near Naples, its waters have been taken by Julius Caesar, Virgil, Michelangelo and Giuseppi Verdi!

Ferrarelle is naturally carbonated — absolutely naturally. **Perrier** is "naturally carbonated," but the carbon dioxide is taken from the water and then re-injected, to maintain a uniform level. **Ferrarelle**, however, is sold just as it comes from the source.

Even on special sales, **Ferrarelle**, in 30 ounce bottles, sells for 99 cents. But we made a special buy, which we can sell for only 59 cents.

Ramlosa, Calistoga, Banning Springs, San Pellegrino and Volvic

Where's Crystal Geyser on the list? This family-run company didn't get its start until 1990.

The Quest for Grapeness

Take a look at the simple goodness in Pilgrim Joe's Concord grape juice. This small-batch, limited edition juice—and the story—is the stuff of farm stands or "craft beverage makers."

Trader Joe's writes about this "endangered species" with a strong reminder: Fresh juice made with amazing fruit is unbeatable.

Here in this little pocket of California, TJ's was powering its quest to keep interesting foods alive just as the Slow Food movement set out to do in 1986. Meanwhile TJ's was urging customers to just say no to frozen, concentrated.

Seasonal drinks like Trader Joe's Unfiltered Honey Crisp Apple Juice keep this tradition of freshly pressed juice alive today.

An endangered species . . .
100% CONCORD GRAPE JUICE 1981 HARVEST

For some reason, **Welch's**, the most famous name in Concord grape juice, has abandoned the field. **Welch's** now claims to be only "grape juice."

One year ago we introduced **Pilgrim Joe's** 100% Concord from the 1980 harvest. It was a raving success, and sold out. Customers demanded more — but we could not satisfy them.

The reason is that **Pilgrim Joe's** is fresh packed from whole Concord grapes, within hours after the harvest. Most other "grape juices" are made from frozen concentrate which can be whistled up from cold storage to meet current demand. **Pilgrim Joe's** is made only once, and when it runs out, there is no more until the next harvest. (1982).

Pilgrim Joe's has some other claims: It is unfiltered (so it may throw a slight deposit.) It is also unsweetened — only the natural grape sugars are present.

We're selling a half gallon for $2.29. **Welch's**, in 40 ounces, sells for the equivalent of $2.38 to $2.78 in the supers.

Note: our product is called "Pilgrim" because the Concord is one of the native American flora discovered here by the Pilgrims.

Serious Cocoa

Hershey's cocoa and Nestlé Quik were the big powdered chocolate products on the scene in 1982. That is until you walked into Trader Joe's. You see this bargain-priced cocoa from Europe for less than the price of domestic cocoa, (as the flyer so ably points out…or screams, at the top of the product description).

What's even cooler than the Trader landing a 4,200-tin cocoa purchase is that Van Houten is the Godfather of cocoa. Coenraad Van Houten invented the hydraulic cocoa press to separate cocoa butter from cocoa powder. Without his cocoa invention, we would be a nation longing for cocoa powder, cocoa-dusted chocolate-covered almonds, and brownie mix, not to mention good chocolate bars![21]

Grape Heavens

If only we could time travel to taste this Unfermented Zinfandel Juice. Interestingly, you now can find juice like this for sale for the purpose of making wine. Is that what customers who innocently bought juice did with this little TJ's treasure? Hmm.

[20] Discover more on the history of cocoa and chocolate in Susie Wyshak's middle-grade book: ChocolateChipCookieSchool.com

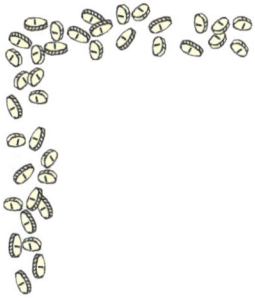

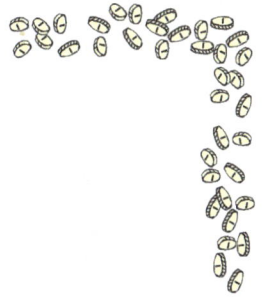

For the Health of It

Thanks, Trader Darwin

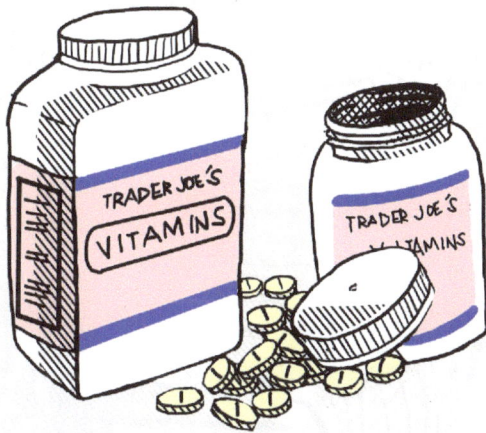

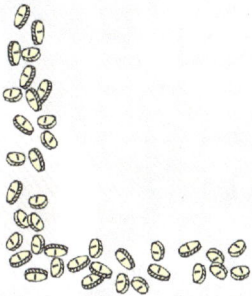

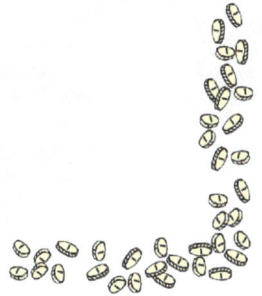

Good Health In a Pill

Was the World Ready?

Protein from Algae
SPIRULINA:
Save the Green at Trader Joe's

Spirulina is the newest fad in the health food business. A rich source of easily digested protein, Spirulina is blue-green micro-algae. In a sense, therefore, it's a food of the future, as the planet will have to turn to algae and plankton increasingly, for food.

Spirulina is also a food of the ancient past: the Aztecs doted on it — and to this day Mexico is the best source of Spirulina (ours is from Lake Texcoco, a big alkaline lake near Mexico City which is famous for its Spirulina).

Unlike other single-celled algae, there's no cellulose in the walls of the cells of Spirulina — making it easier to digest. Spirulina contains all eight essential amino acids. It is very high in Vitamin B 12 (which is hard to get in a vegetarian diet). Spirulina is also rich in Vitamin A, and has many trace elements, including iron. (The Vitamin A is provitamin A, the type which is not associated with toxic build-up in the body.)

Tablets of Spirulina usually sell for $7.49 to $12.49 (per 100 tablets of 500 milligrams). Even on sale, it goes for $5.49. But **Trader Darwin's** Spirulina is only $3.99 — the lowest price any place.

Because this is a food of both the past and the future, we call it **Trader Darwin's Janus Spirulina,** and the label has a picture of Janus, the god who looked both forward and backward.

Protein from Algae?!

Since the dawn of time, or maybe the dawn of fire, people have hunted down more and better protein sources.

And so it was that the Trader Joe's alter ego, Trader Darwin, urged his Southern California fans to give green spirulina algae a try, just for the health of it.

You can still find TD's (Trader Darwin's) spirulina in your nearest vitamin aisle (and in TJ's green smoothie drinks). Today's spirulina tablets have something even better than the old generation—organic certification.

Funnily enough, there's recent talk of algae becoming a major protein source for humankind.[21] In other words, Trader Joe's was way ahead of its time…as usual.

---

[21] For the algae-curious, see *Fast Company:* "Hope You Like Algae, Because It's Going To Be In Everything You Eat" https://www.fastcoexist.com/3067961/hope-you-like-algae-because-its-going-to-be-in-everything-you-eat

When Vitamins Were Just Vitamins

Ever heard the phrase "take your vitamins!"? We hardly ever referred to vitamins by letter, there were so few options. Vitamin D was not a national obsession.

Drug stores and supermarkets did not usually have vitamins under their own store names. You reached for the brand whose TV and print advertising made you confident in that brand.

Gummy bears were something you found in the candy aisle—not vitamins disguised as yummy fruit chews.

Will you risk vitamins labeled with a store brand? The flyer explains that the Trader's low prices come not from low quality, but from TJ's knack of wrangling the best deal possible, direct from the manufacturer. We'll take their vitamins.

Lowest Price Anywhere: TIME RELEASE VITAMIN C $6.19

We sell 250 tablets of Time Release Vitamin C for only $6.19. Each contains 1000 milligrams of C. All the C is derived from natural sources. No sugar, starch, artificial preservatives, coloring or flavoring have been used.

At our competitors, comparable product sells for $12.99 to $18.99 off the shelf. On "sale" it's sold for $8.99 to $10.99.

Our price is so low, because we buy direct from the manufacturer, in quantities of millions, and we operate on a much thinner margin than health food stores.

(The next time you're in one of those covered shopping malls, consider how much rent the health food stores there are paying. It's murder! They have to charge more, just to pay the rent!)

How would you like to pay the rent in a covered Mahal?

NATURAL VITAMIN E

Here we have **Trader Darwin's** Natural Vitamin E, in capsules of 200 International Unit strength, at only $1.69 for a bottle of 100 capsules.

The lowest price we can find at our competitors for similar product is $2.99, with most health food stores charging $5.75.

This Vitamin E is d-Alpha Tocopherol with other tocopherols that normally come with the d-Alpha in nature (beta, gamma, and delta.) The source is soybean and wheat germ oil.

We have sold out of the 1000 International Unit capsule offered in the October *Insider's Report*, and our quantity of the 200 I.U. capsules is limited.

Finally, Cheap Natural Dog Food

Good For All. Woof!

Your best friend is not left behind in the quest for better-for-you foods. One glance at this kibble description, and you'll be ready to start chowing down yourself!

Trader Joe's Kibble Fills all the Nutritional Standards for Dogs

"If you compare what people buy and what an animal needs, it is shocking. Look for a 'Nutritional Guarantee.' It means the product meets the standards for growth and reproduction set by the National Research Council, the same governmental body that sets human nutrition standards."

John L. Mara, doctor of veterinary medicine and veterinary consultant, in the **Los Angeles Times**, January 4, 1982

One of our most successful products is **Trader Joe's Kibble**. Little wonder: we sell a 25 pound bag for $6.99. The same formula sells in pet specialty stores for twice as

much. And even **Ralston Purina** dog chow sells for $8.15 in the supers.

If you'll look on our label, you'll find the National Research Council specifications — 25 different aspects of doggy nutrition — and how **Trader Joe's Kibble** exceeds all of these requirements.

We also urge you to read the ingredients statement on our label — especially look for what is **not** there. Like corn is not there (it's hard to digest). Nor soybean protein (ditto). Nor artificial coloring, preservatives, etc.

Why We Love Trader Joe's

Times May Have Changed. Our Passion Has Not!

TJ's Then & Now
1982

The Secret: Trader Joe's Loves Us

It's Not Rocket Science

This 1982 flyer is a remarkable peek into a young company that's managed to stay true to its roots despite growing nearly 16 times to more than 450 stores today.

You'd never know a quirky sea-faring adventurer wasn't behind the helm of this bell-ringing store. Yet this is the secret behind great businesses: Focus on making customers as happy as can be.

How did they do it? The flyer quotes Carl Sagan and, in doing so, answers this very question:

Another answer to "What is a Businessman?" might be: Someone who connects the dots to create value. In the case of Trader Joe's, the businessman who connected the dots to create a company we love was Joe Coulombe, the founder of Trader Joe's.

Joe's principles keep us coming back for amazing foods, welcoming staff, and clever packaging innovations.

Trader Joe's satisfies our desires for reliability with a dash of excitement— the secret sauce in all great relationships.

What is a Businessman?

"Businessmen are a special breed," says Sagan wryly. "It takes certain skills that even famous academics might not have."

— Carl Sagan, quoted in **Science**, January 8, 1982 on his failing venture called The Cosmos Store.

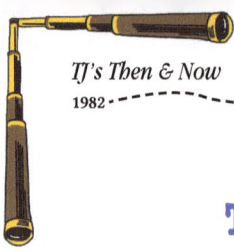

TJ's Truly Changed the Way America Eats

Imagine life without Trader Joe's. Would you be so open to new foods? Would you involuntarily rave about your food discoveries?

This flyer reveals the amazing way a young Trader Joe's led us to become a nation of adventurous health-foodies. What you saw in the flyer still remains the open secret to the Cult of TJ's today:

1. **Limit choices** for each type of food. Ever get paralyzed trying to choose the right nut butter at a Trader Joe's? Probably not very often considering you only have a handful to choose from…and they're all just different enough. A lot of thought and research went into the idea of limiting choice. This is by design. Coulombe analysed how a successful grocer, Stew Leonard, raked in $100 million in sales per year in only one store while selling far fewer products than the typical supermarket.[22]

2. **Keep prices low**, by buying direct and in huge quantities[23] while keeping logistics simple.

3. **Focus on food that's delicious, interesting and better for you**. Lots of companies are just starting to say "no" to artificial ingredients and preservatives. TJ's charted the course.

Beyond Amazing Food

It was Tax Day 2017. I stood in line with only 2 pieces of aged cheese. The man behind me had only wine. "We should have a party together!" I said. "Ya, all we need is bread," he said, raising his wine. The woman in front of me chimed in: "I've got meatballs. Can I come?" We all laughed. I don't know about you, but these sorts of interchange never happen at other grocery stores. The spirit of TJ's leads to community, Tax Day or not.

---

[22] George Anderson, "Why Are Trader Joe's Customers the Most Satisfied in America?", *Forbes* https://www.forbes.com/sites/retailwire/2013/07/30/why-are-trader-joes-customers-the-most-satisfied-in-america/#1c8ac7131ea0 (July 30, 2013)

[23] David Gura, "Trader Joe's Successful But Secretive", NPR

[24] Beth Kowitt, "Meet the Original Joe", Fortune.com
http://features.blogs.fortune.cnn.com/2010/08/23/meet-the-original-joe/?iid=EL (August 23, 2010)

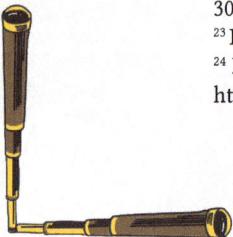

A Good Business Person Fosters Leaders

Meet Doug Rauch

The 1982 flyer mentioned buyer Doug Rauch several times, a practice you rarely see in grocery store promotions.

This young employee thrived at Trader Joe's. During 31-years at TJ's, Doug was the primary force (with Joe Coulombe) in creating their private-label food program. Doug then became the sole National President for the last several years before retiring.

The Next Chapter

I had the chance to meet Doug at his amazing not-for-profit store, Daily Table. This grocery store makes fresh meals and healthy packaged food very affordable to very low-income folks. (See DailyTable.org)

Trader Joe's stores also help the hungry—an estimated 1 in 6 Americans[25]—with lots of local food donations.

And so our food adventure concludes with a big thanks to Trader Joe's for spicing up our meals, our conversations, and our lives. TJ's truly changed the way America eats!

THIS BOOK DOES GOOD

A portion of profits from this book will be donated to food banks and to the non-profit Daily Table grocery store.

---

[25] DoSomething: https://www.dosomething.org/facts/11-facts-about-hunger-us

About the Author

Susie Wyshak

They say do what you loved in your youth. Seeking out Trader Joe's stores is a life-long love, since my childhood in Southern California in the early 80s. Discovering great foods and sharing food stories is another. To help aspiring food entrepreneurs, I wrote *Good Food, Great Business: How to Take Your Artisan Food Idea From Concept to Marketplace* (Chronicle Books).

My second book *Chocolate Chip Cookie School* helps kids learn critical thinking through cookies, by deconstructing the history of the cookie and its ingredients, then learning how to plan a cookie business or bake sale.

Download a fun, free Trader Joe's Chocolate Chip Cookie Critical Thinking comparison exercise—where you compare 2 types of TJ's chocolate chip cookies—at ChocolateChipCookieSchool.com

LET'S CONNECT AND & SHARE OUR LOVE FOR TRADER JOE'S

Email me at susie@foodstarter.com if you have early So. Cal. memories to share or other ideas for collaboration.

Join in on the TJ's history conversation at TraderJoesHistory.com

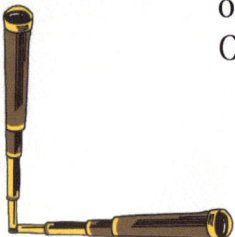

www.ingramcontent.com/pod-product-compliance
Lightning Source LLC
Chambersburg PA
CBHW061355090426
42739CB00003B/37